Preface

Mother nature provides us with many playthings that change with the seasons. One of my very favorites is the fields and meadows that are filled with wildflowers. They are so inviting to walk through and children love to run and play amongst them.

Daisies and clovers are abundant everywhere and you don't need a field or meadow full of these little beauties to have some fun with them. They are found along the roadside in the park as well as your back yard. Gather up and handful of them and find a comfortable and shady spot to make some of the things shown in this book. All you need is some string and a small pair of scissors.

Spending some quality time with your young ones, teaching them how to make these wonderful things, you will get them away from the video games, teach them how to use their hands and pass on a love for nature, all while creating cherished memories for both of you that will last forever. They will think of you whenever they see a cluster of daisies or clovers and remember the day you crowned them a Daisy Princesses or Clover Blossom Fairy.

The instructions in this book are simple and laid out step by step so they are easy to follow. You don't need any special tools, to make these pieces. You can even use long blades of grass in place of string.

Daisies

Daisies are wonderful and beautiful flowers. Many grow wild and have common names such as Lawn Daisy, Common Daisy or English Daisy. You can find them growing in vast numbers in fields and meadows in many places around the world. Some will reach your waist, if you are a little girl and grow on strong tall stems. If you are bigger then a little girl they will reach up above your knees.

Most everyone knows how to pluck the little petals off a daisy to the saying she loves me, she loves me not, she loves me.

But there is so much more you can do with them.

How to Make A Daisy Crown

Collect a bunch of daisies with long stems. Long stems are easy to work with but they can be much longer then needed, you can trim them as needed. You can keep them as "fresh as a daisy" by putting them into a bucket of water. Daisies respond quickly to a drink.

The first thing you should do is strip off any leaves from the stems, put the leaves back in the bucket with water so they stay fresh, you can use the leaves once your crown is complete to dress it up and add some fullness.

Step 1 – Hold your first daisy **(marked A)** horizontally as shown in the **Step 1** picture below. Then add your second daisy **(marked B)** vertically over the daisy **A's** stem. Position daisy **B** so that the petals of daisy **B** are about one quarter to one half inch back from daisy **A's** flower head.

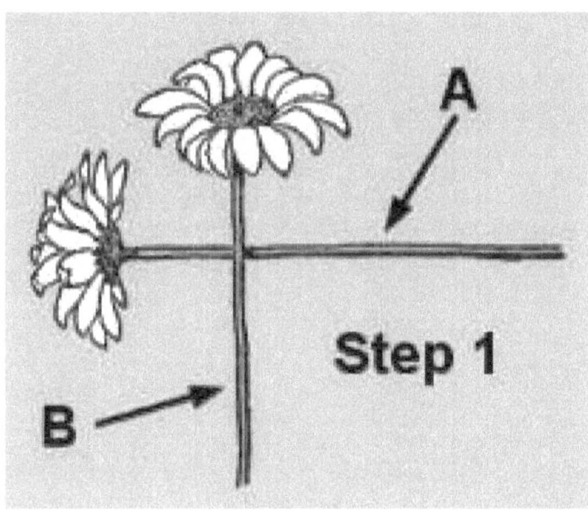

Step 2 – Hold the intersection of the two stems between your fingers as you use your other hand to turn the stem of daisy **B** under the stem of daisy **A** as shown in **Step 2** picture below.

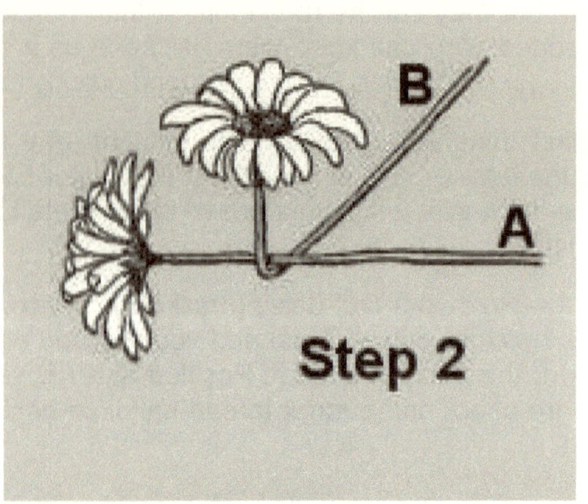

Step 3 – Bring stem **B** snugly around stem **A** and over stem **B** as shown in **Step 3**.

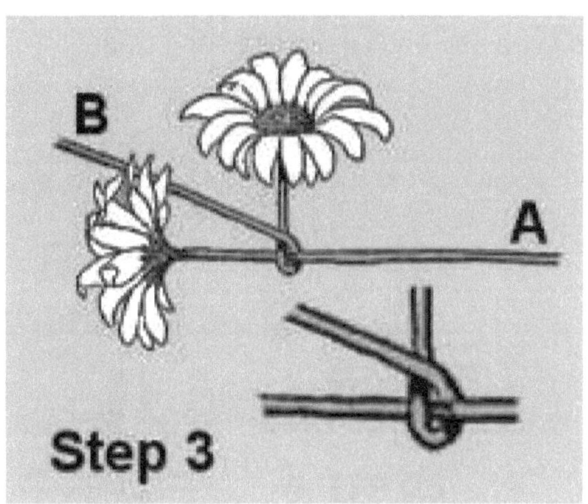

Step 4 – Continue bending stem **B** all the way around stem **B** so looks like the wrap shown in the close up of **Step 4**. Lay the stems snugly against each other; I left some space between the stems in the picture so you can see each stem plain and clear.

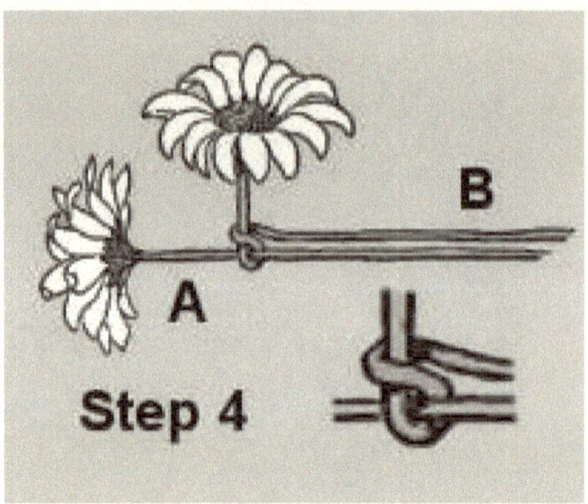

Step 5 – Now add the next daisy, daisy **C**. Position daisy **C** so that the petals touch the petals of daisy **B**, they will spread out a little as you curve your crown into its final shape. Repeat steps 2, 3 and 4 by wrapping stems **A** and **B** with stem **C** as shown in **Step 5** below.

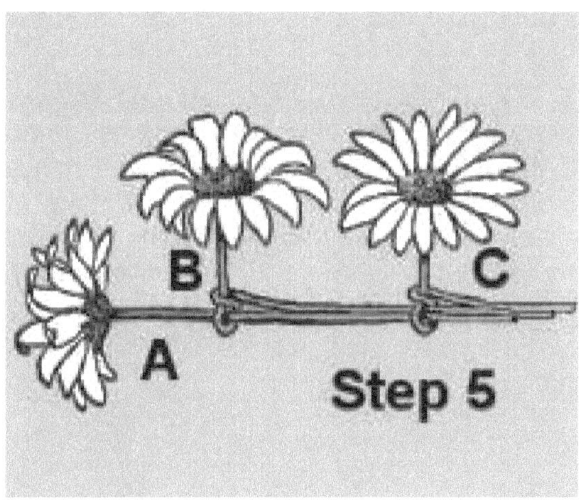

Keep your wraps sung but not so tight that you break stems. After you add 4 or 5 daisies you will come to the end of stem **A** depending on how long the stem is. It would make your work become too bulky if you are wrapping more the 4 or 5 stems at a time, so if you come to that point anywhere in your work you can simply trim off stem as required.

Step 6 - Once you have added enough flowers to make it long enough to wrap around and fit your or your little princesses head you can trim off the extra stems, leaving about 3 inches of stems. Use some string or fishing line or even a length of daisy stem to tie up the ends of the stems snugly and tie those ends to the daisy **A** stem just under the flower to complete your daisy crown as shown in **Step 6** below.

At this point you can add in some of the daisy leaves or ferns or any other green leaves you like the look of to fill out the crown. You can even weave in some other types of flowers you like. Just slip the stems of what you want to add between the stems of the daisies and weave them in with one or two wraps to keep them in place.

The daisy chain you made can be used for many things; it does not have to be a crown. A small wreath can dress up a candle or tossed in the pool to add some movement and color, several of these floating around in a pool is a very pretty sight. You can use a long daisy chain to dress up your picnic table or shade umbrella, how about a heart wreath to dress up your door or garden gate. Let your imagination go!

Clovers

Clovers grow everywhere and in many different colors, they are commonly call red or white clovers. Red clovers are typically lavender or purple in color, there is a crimson clover that is an intense red color but they are not as wide spread as the red or white clover blossoms. They grow wild in fields and parks and in your yard. Clovers that do not get cut have longer stems then those found in yards and parks because the clovers in our yards and parks are cut when the grass is cut so they adapt and bloom on shorter stems. Some on a single stem and others grow on spindly stems with several blooms, these spindly stem clovers are easier to work with just because of the longer stems, but all can be used to make the following items. Mix or match colors any way you like.

Clover Blossom Bracelet

Gather lots of clovers, the longer the stems are the easier they are to work with. You will need some light string or fishing line or even some long blades of grass to wrap the stems with as you make your bracelet.

To make anything with clover blossoms it is easier to make small bundles of clovers first, and then use the bundles to make your bracelet. You use this same method to make a necklace, headband or crown. First decide what you are going to make then determine how thin or thick you want your clover item to be. In the pictures and example below we use three flowers or blossoms per bundle, which is a good size for a bracelet, but if you wanted a thicker wreath you can make it a six-blossom bundle. As we build the item it is called a chain until the ends are joined and then it is a bracelet, wreath or what ever else you are making.

Step 1 – Select the clovers for the first bundle and gather the stems close together and laying in a straight line and wrap the stems with string binding them together to make a neat bundle that is easy to work with as shown in the pictures below. Tie the string off at the end of the bundle so they don't come loose.

The picture above shows everything loose for illustration purposes. The picture below is how your bundle will look when complete. You do not need as many wraps as shown in the pictures, 3 to 5 wraps depending on how long the stems are. The string does not have to be very tight, just enough to hold the stems together snugly.

Step 2 – Continue making these bundles until your have enough to assemble them together to make the length of clover chain you need which will vary in length depending on what you are making.

Step 3 – This is where you assemble your individual bundles into a chain. Use the same technique as you did to make the bundle. Lay the stems of the bundles close together, position the flowers close to the first bunch but not over lapping and bind them together by wrapping string around their stems. When two bundles are wrapped add a third bundle then fourth until your clover chain is long enough to wrap around your wrist.

Step 4 – Once you have the chain long enough to make the bracelet, shape it into a circle and over lap the stems of the last bunch with the stems of the first bunch and make a few more wraps with the string to secure the ends together, tie the string and trim any loose stems. You are done!

Clover Blossom Necklace

To make a necklace all you do is make a longer clover chain. Repeat the instructions for making the bracelet; the only difference is the length of clover chain. Six to eight inches may have been enough for a bracelet but twelve to fifteen inches for a necklace.

If you do decide on a necklace you can add a pendant to make it even more special. If you want to add a pendant do not join the ends of the clover chain yet. First make a pendant and then join the pendant ends to each end of the chain with the same method of winding the string around binding the clover pendant to the clover chain and tying the string around the joined ends.

Clover Pendant

To make the pendant select three nice clover blossoms and arrange them as shown in the picture below.

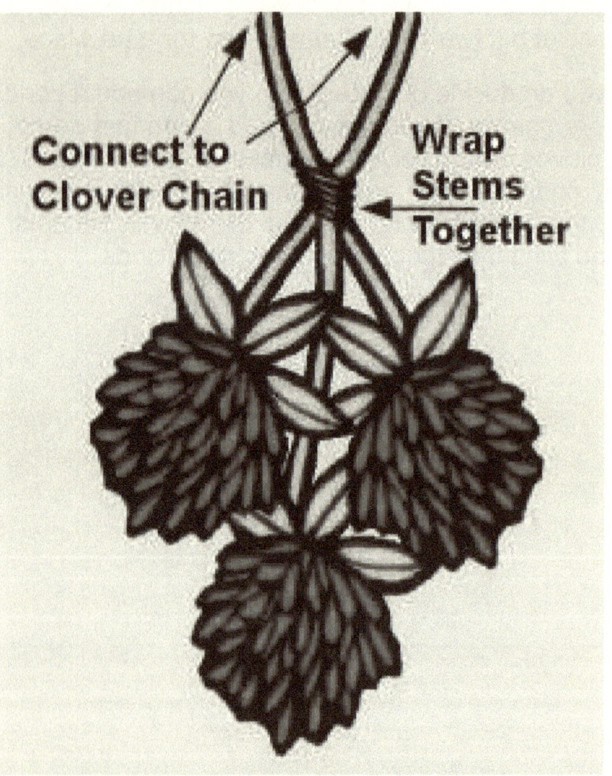

Wrap the stems about 2 inches above the flowers so they keep their shape. In the picture above you see two stems marked "connect to clover chain" you can add some clover leaves or just extra stems to give them some added strength or length if needed. Wrap them the same way you did when you bundled the stems together for the chain. Position the stem ends of the pendant on the clover chain and tie them in place the same way. Be sure to tie both ends of the pendant into the chain so there is equal length stem between the chain and pendant on both sides so the pendant hangs straight. Now you have a stylish clover blossom necklace to go with your daisy crown and clover bracelet.

Clover Blossom Ring

A ring will complete the look for any princesses and is very easy to make and looks great! Simply pick the finest clover-blossom to be the jewel of the ring. Place it on the finger you wish then wrap the stem around your finger back up the flower. Then wrap the stem around the stem right under the flower head as shown in the picture below. Bring the loose end of the stem back down and tuck in under the stem that is wrapped around your finger 2 or 3 times and trim off the loose end.

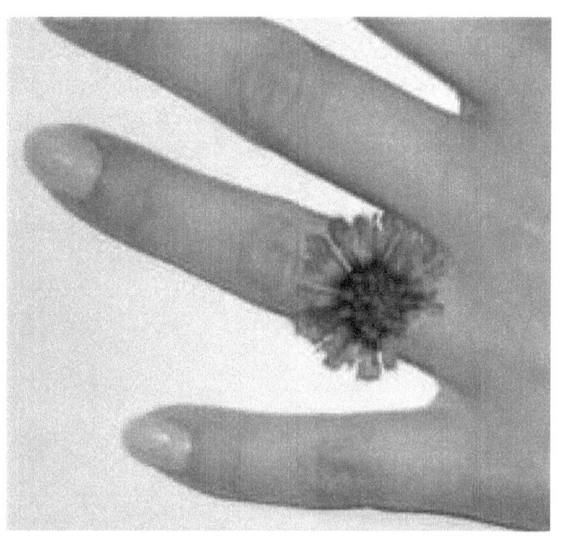

Clovers can also be used as floaters in your pool. You can use them with leaves or without. Leave some stem on the clovers when you put them in the water, it helps keep them stable and floating upright.

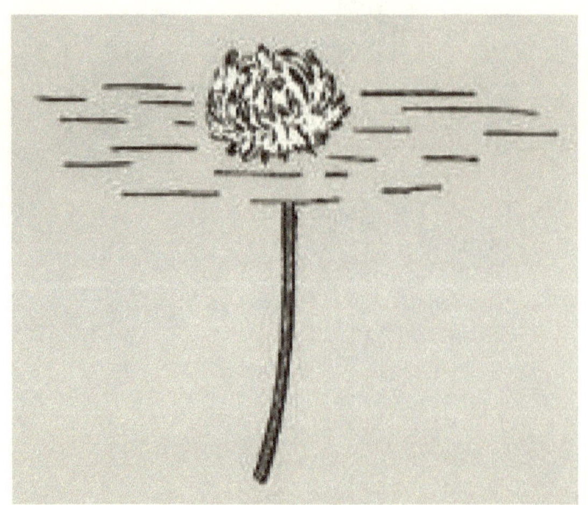

The End